The Roger Evans BEGINNERS GUITAR BOOK

This book explains everything you need to know to begin playing the guitar. Simply follow the easy instructions and start making your own music.

The Beginners Guitar Book is the result of many years playing and teaching the guitar. I hope the benefit of my experience will introduce you to all of the pleasures of guitar playing.

Roger Evans

New Edition
First Published 1984

© EMI Music Publishing Ltd
127 Charing Cross Road, London WC2H 0EA

Exclusive Distributors
International Music Publications
Southend Road, Woodford Green,
Essex IG8 8HN.

Introduction to the Guitar

There are several different instruments in the guitar family, but the most common, and the one which concerns us here, is the six-stringed guitar. This is the most versatile and widely used guitar and can have either steel or nylon strings.

Originally all guitars were acoustic, that is they were designed to produce their own sound. Today many instruments use a magnetic pick-up and an amplifier to produce an 'electric' sound. This is only possible using steel strings.

Generally, if a guitar is to be used on it's own or for accompanying solo singing it can be used un-amplified (acoustic), but if it is to be used in a group or band an amplifier is required. This doesn't mean that you need an amplifier in order to learn to play, even though you wish to join a group when you have become proficient. There are many steel strung guitars to which a pick-up can be added when required.

The Parts of the Guitar

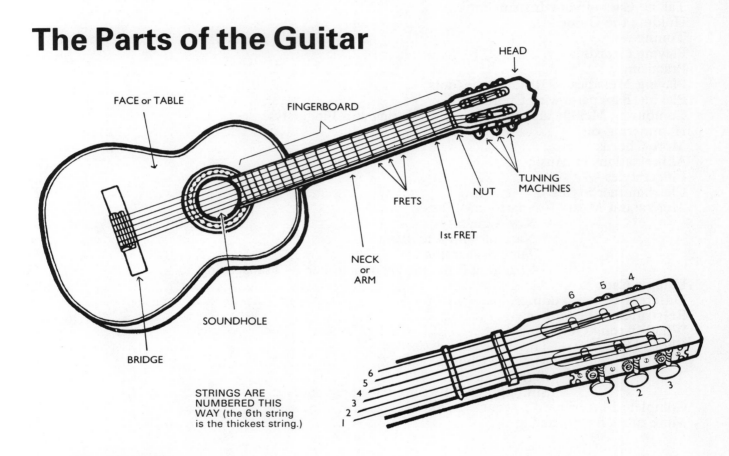

NYLON STRINGS

The 1st, 2nd and 3rd strings are usually made of single strand nylon while the 4th, 5th and 6th are a thin strand of nylon wound with silver or bronze plated copper wire.

STEEL STRINGS

The 1st and 2nd strings are usually plain nickel-plated steel while the 3rd, 4th, 5th and 6th are wound with wire.

DON'T put steel strings on a guitar made for nylon strings as the extra tension will strain the instrument. This could warp the neck, pull the bridge off or cause the guitar to literally pull itself to pieces.

Different types of Guitar

Choose the one most suitable for the type of music you wish to play.

1. NYLON STRUNG GUITARS

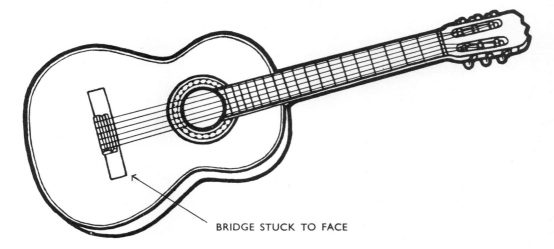

BRIDGE STUCK TO FACE

These are played fingerstyle (the sounds are produced by hitting the strings with the fingers of the right hand). In addition to being used for Classical and Flamenco (Spanish) music they are also used for accompanying singing. They produce a more mellow tone than steel strung instruments and although they are easier on the left hand fingers the neck is wide and this requires somewhat longer fingers than a 'Folk style' guitar.

2. STEEL STRUNG GUITARS

2a Roundhole Guitars. These include: 'Jumbos', 'Dreadnoughts', Country and Western, Folk Style, etc., and can be played fingerstyle, with finger picks or with a plectrum.

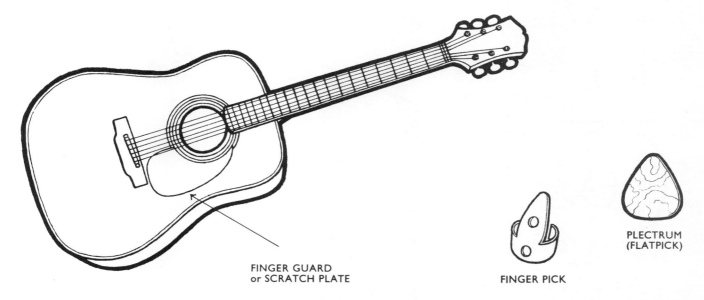

FINGER GUARD
or SCRATCH PLATE

FINGER PICK

PLECTRUM
(FLATPICK)

They are good, general purpose guitars and can be used for folksongs, country and western, blues, rhythm playing. Some are used in groups with pick-ups added and played through amplifiers.

2b Cello Guitars. They are generally played with a plectrum either acoustically or amplified. They produce a 'chunky' rhythm sound which is characteristic and are found in Dance Bands, Pop and Jazz Groups.

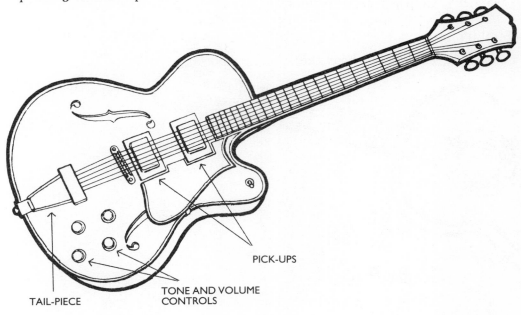

PICK-UPS

TONE AND VOLUME
CONTROLS

TAIL-PIECE

Some cello guitars are only about $1\frac{1}{2}$ inches thick and these are called 'Semi-Acoustics'. They are always used amplified, but on their own produce enough sound for practising. They give a better tone than 'solid' guitars when used amplified and are not as heavy.

2c Solid Guitars are for amplified use only because they make virtually no sound on their own. They are usually played with a plectrum and are less liable to make unwanted electronic noises than other types of amplified guitars. Solid guitars can be any shape or style, however they need high quality pick-ups to give a good sound.

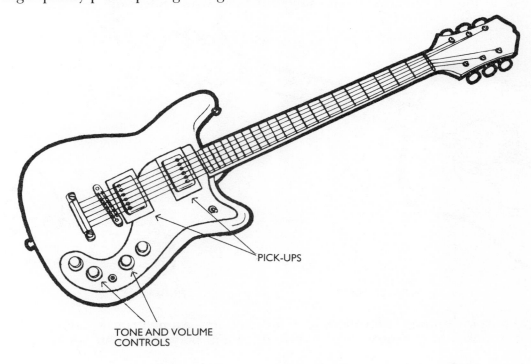

PICK-UPS

TONE AND VOLUME
CONTROLS

Buying your Guitar

This can be a bit of a problem unless you know a lot about guitars. It's a good idea to get an experienced guitarist or teacher to help you select a suitable instrument, as some salesmen will have no qualms about selling you an instrument which is quite unsuitable. Don't be afraid to ask the advice of an experienced musician—he will usually be only too pleased to help if he can.

Decide which type of guitar you require and bear the following points in mind:

1. Don't be tempted to buy a very expensive instrument until you can play quite well. It is possible to buy a fairly inexpensive guitar which will be as easy to play and will suit you for quite a while.

2. Unless you have someone very experienced with you don't be tempted by 'bargains' in second-hand shops—your 'bargain' could turn out to be useless and expensive.

3. If possible ask someone to tune and play the instrument for you. If either are difficult for him, beware; you could have the same trouble.

IS ANYTHING WRONG WITH IT?
Check:
1. That the fingerboard is straight. Do this by sighting along it or laying a straight edge along it.

2. That the action is not too high. This is the height of the strings above the fingerboard. If too high it will be difficult to play. At the twelfth fret it should be no more than about $\frac{1}{4}$-inch. On most instruments it is less.

3. That all frets are the same height.

4. That all six strings are on it and that the tuning machines all work. If not, have them fixed before you buy the guitar.

5. That when played there are no rattles or buzzes—this could mean structural damage.

Note: If in doubt about any of the parts mentioned see page 2, 'Parts of the Guitar'.

Taking Care of your Instrument

A guitar is a comparatively fragile instrument and if you want it to remain in one piece and in good condition you should take care of it. Keep and carry it around in a strong case, preferably a hard one (made of wood or fibreglass) for an expensive instrument. It is advisable to keep it out of the way of clumsy hands and feet—on top of, or inside a wardrobe or some such place. Don't leave it near a radiator or in the sun, even in its case.

When you've finished playing, clean the strings by running a cloth along them, underneath as well as on top. This will make them last longer.

Holding the Guitar

This is a generally, fairly comfortable position. A Flamenco or classical guitarist would usually not cross his legs but support the guitar on his left leg, which is raised by using a small stool.

However, the position shown would be acceptable to most people. Note that the guitar is held upright and not flat on the lap. Although it is harder to see the fingerboard you will find your left hand fingering much easier in this position.

THE LEFT HAND

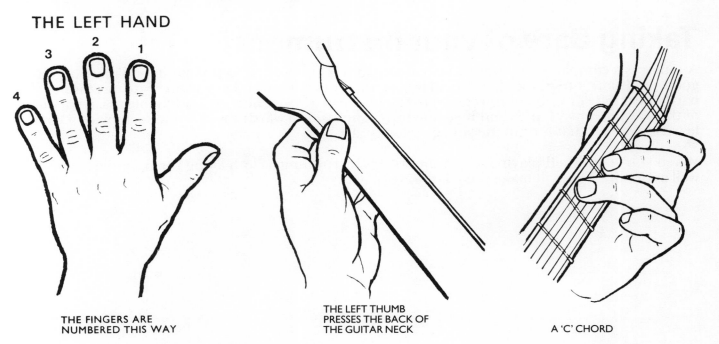

THE FINGERS ARE
NUMBERED THIS WAY

THE LEFT THUMB
PRESSES THE BACK OF
THE GUITAR NECK

A 'C' CHORD

The nails on the left hand should be kept short and not project past the tips of the fingers.

THE RIGHT HAND

For the purposes of finger styles the fingers are numbered as follows:

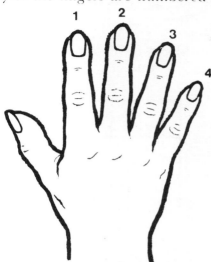

It is also possible to use the thumb on its own as an alternative to using a combination of the thumb and fingers. The finger nails on this hand can be grown longer.

USING A PLECTRUM

For some styles a plectrum is used (but never on nylon strings as this would damage them). Choose one that is fairly stiff but not completely rigid. Grip it firmly between your thumb and 1st finger. The best way to hold it is like this:

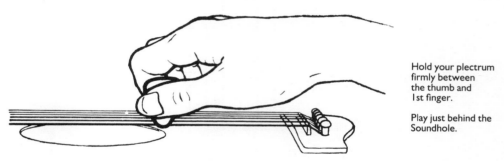

Hold your plectrum firmly between the thumb and 1st finger.

Play just behind the Soundhole.

Tuning

It is usual to tune the guitar using the frets after tuning the 1st string to the 'E' above 'middle C'. You can get this note from a piano or another instrument or from a pitch pipe. Usually pitch pipes give all the notes for the six strings and as you can buy one cheaply this is the best way to start. When you have your 1st string in tune the remainder are tuned as follows:

Press the second string just behind the 5th fret and turn its tuning machine until it makes the same sound as the first string 'open'. A string is 'open' when it isn't fingered. Then tune the others by:

Pressing the 3rd string at the 4th fret and tuning to the 2nd string.
Pressing the 4th string at the 5th fret and tuning to the 3rd string.
Pressing the 5th string at the 5th fret and tuning to the 4th string.
Pressing the 6th string at the 5th fret and tuning to the 5th string.

Even though you may have tuned all strings from pitch pipes it is advisable to check by the frets. It is worth taking time to tune-up properly as however little you can play, it will sound better if the guitar is properly tuned.

Playing Chords

A chord is a collection of two or more notes that are played together. For accompanying purposes it is usual to play at least four notes together (this is what is called a four-note chord) as this gives a fuller sound. It is usual to use symbols (C, G7, etc.) to name different chords.

For reference they are usually shown in blocks or 'chord diagrams'. The vertical lines show the strings and the horizontal lines the frets, like this:

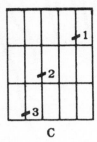

C

This chord is called 'C'. The dots show the position of the fingers and the numbers tell you which finger to use. Here the 1st finger of the left hand is placed on the 2nd string just behind the first fret; the 2nd finger on the 4th string just behind the second fret and the 3rd finger on the 5th string behind the third fret. When your fingers are in place press from behind with your thumb. Then play the chord by stroking the thumb of your right hand across the strings.

Now try this other chord which is called G7:

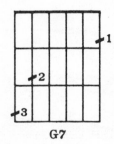

G7

CHANGING CHORDS

Most beginners find it awkward to change from one chord to another, but if you try everything slowly at first you will soon find it easier. Try changing from C to G7 and back again to C, playing each chord once. When you can do this fairly smoothly try playing each chord twice before changing. This would be written like this:

| C   ∕ | G7   ∕ | C   ∕ |

The strokes after the chord names tell you to repeat that chord. The vertical lines which separate the two beats are called bar lines and are used to break up the music into easily read pieces. When you play two beats between each bar line it is called '2 to the bar'. Four to the bar (also called four-four or Common Time) is written like this:

| C   ∕ ∕ ∕ | G7   ∕ ∕ ∕ | C   ∕ ∕ ∕ | etc.

Try to change your chords without missing a beat. You could try tapping your foot to keep the time. Now try to play these chords (four to the bar) to accompany the tune 'Skip to my Lou'.

| C / / / | C / / / | G7 / / / | G7 / · / / |
She's gone a - gain____ Skip to my Lou, She's gone a - gain____ Skip to my Lou, She's

| C / / / · | C / / / | G7 / / / | C / / / |
gone a - gain____ Skip to my Lou, Skip to my Lou, my Dar - ling

I have put the words in position against the chords so you can see how they fit in.

PRACTISING

It is better to do a little practice every day (say about 20 minutes) than to put in several hours at one stretch. Try to learn one piece properly before trying something new in the same style. If you have difficulty with one style it is often a good idea to try something completely different and then come back and **practise** the more awkward piece. For example, if you find chord changing difficult at first, **practise** it a little and then try playing melody as an alternative (see page 11). When you have tried this come back to your chord changes.

MORE CHORDS

Besides having 'major' chords like 'C' there are also 'minor' chords. These are distinguished by a small 'm' after the chord name. Try playing 'Am' to 'Dm' to 'Am' (see below) and compare with the sound of 'C' to 'G7'. In modern harmony minor chords are often used to add interest to a chord sequence.

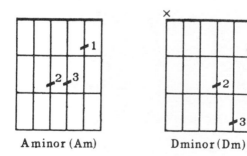

Aminor (Am)   Dminor (Dm)

Note that the 6th string on the 'Dm' chord has a small 'x' above it. This means that this string should not be played, so start your stroke from the 5th string.

Try playing them in this order: C Am Dm G7 C and **practise** until you can play the changes smoothly.
Note that to change from C to Am only one finger need move. When changing from Dm to G7 leave the 1st finger where it is.
These chords are often used in the following patterns and occur in such songs as: 'Blue Moon', 'Moonlight in Vermont', 'La Mer', 'Where Have All the Flowers Gone' and many more.

| C / Am / | Dm / G7 / | C / / / | Am / / / | Dm / / / | G7 / / / |

Normally these sequences would be repeated several times in a song but they should be finished by playing a 'C' chord. Generally speaking, a tune should not end on a '7th' chord as it won't sound finished. Try it and see how it sounds. 'G7' is used to lead a sequence back to 'C'. These chords have been included early on in the book as they are all fairly easy to play and appear in many tunes. However, there is one more chord that must be learned before more tunes are attempted. This is called 'F'.

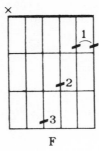

F

To play this chord the 1st finger should cover both the 1st and 2nd strings. This will seem awkward at first, but try it this way: Put your 1st finger on the 2nd string as you would to play a 'C' chord; then put your 2nd and 3rd fingers in place and by slightly twisting your hand and flattening your 1st finger press it down on the 1st string as well. It may not sound very clearly at first, but keep on trying and you will suddenly find that you have mastered it. When playing an 'F' chord remember not to hit the 6th string.

Try changing chords in this order:
1. C F C G7
2. C F G7 C
When you can change chords smoothly try this tune.

JIMMY CRACK CORN

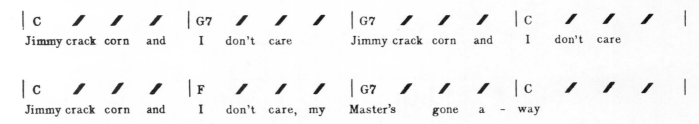

The next tune is in Waltz time. This has three beats to the bar instead of the usual four.

ON TOP OF OLD SMOKEY

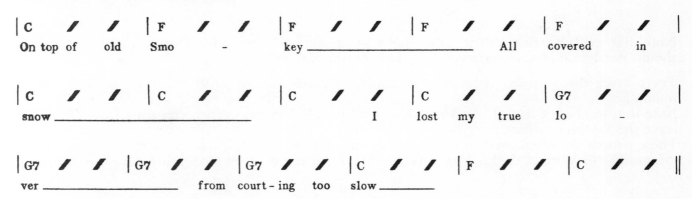

Notice how some of the words carry over several beats.

Playing Melodies

It is possible to play melodies 'by ear', but for most people it is easier to learn to read a little music. This is not as difficult as you might think and after learning the basic principles it will be useful to you when playing guitar. Try to learn a little at a time and keep referring back if in doubt.

'READING THE DOTS'

The notes are named from A to G (A, B, C, D, E, F, G). After G you start again at A. This way you will find three or four notes of the same name on the guitar but they will be different in pitch. Both the 6th string and the 1st string played open are called E, but the 1st string sounds much higher. The notes are written on a 'stave' of five lines and the note will change depending on its position on the stave. For example, the note on the bottom line is E, F is in the space above it, G is on the next line up and so on.

The sign 𝄞 at the beginning of the line is 'a treble clef' and occurs on all guitar music.

We will deal first with the notes on the 1st, 2nd and 3rd strings. When played open (not fingered with the left hand) they are written thus:

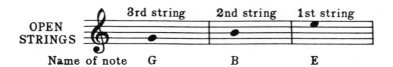

Some other notes on these strings are shown below. The figures above the notes refer to the number of the fret ('o' is open) and also to the number of the finger on the left hand, which is used to play it. Use the 1st finger to play the notes on the first fret, the 2nd finger for the notes on the second fret, etc. Try and play this smoothly before proceeding:

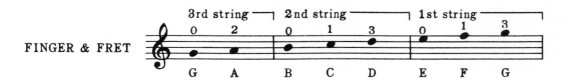

Before playing a simple tune you need to know how to tell the length of each note. This is shown by the way that the note is written. Below are the common ones:

- 𝅝 a whole note.

- 𝅗𝅥 a half note. So, two half notes last as long as one whole note.

- 𝅘𝅥 a quarter note. Two quarter notes last as long as one half note, and four quarter notes last as long as one whole note.

- 𝅘𝅥𝅮 an eighth note. Two or more of these can be joined together like this 𝅘𝅥𝅮𝅘𝅥𝅮

- 𝅘𝅥𝅯 a sixteenth note. Two or more of these can be joined together like this 𝅘𝅥𝅯𝅘𝅥𝅯

DOTTED NOTES

If a note has a dot after it ($\downarrow$.) it lasts half as long again.

The tails of the notes usually go up for notes on the middle line or below and down above that.

etc.

COUNTING THE LENGTH OF EACH NOTE

At the beginning of a piece of music there will be an indication of the number and type of beats

to each bar. or tells you that there are four quarter notes to each bar.

This is the most usual time signature and so it is also called 'Common Time'.

Waltz time, or three quarter notes to the bar, is shown like this:

The best way to get the time of each note right is to count the number of beats to each bar. Here are some examples:

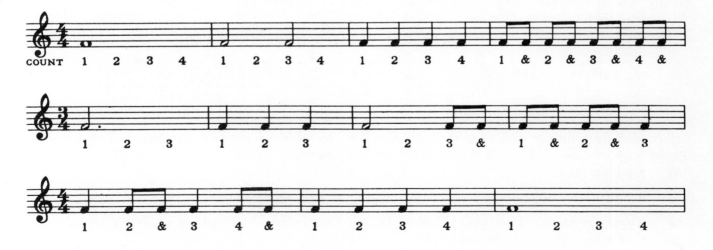

Now you should be ready to play a simple tune. I have repeated the notes of the top three strings so that you can refer to them. By looking them up when necessary you will soon learn them.

OLD MACDONALD'S FARM

Here is another tune to play on the top three strings:

CLAIR DE LUNE (French Folk Song)

Notice that the first, second and fourth lines of this tune are identical. When looking at music always check to see if part of it repeats. It will save you time and trouble as you won't have to work out the same piece again.

14

PLAYING THE 4TH, 5TH, AND 6TH STRINGS

These are written lower down the stave.

The 4th string open is called 'D' and is written here

Notice that it is below the bottom line. 'Leger Lines' are used to continue the stave downwards so that even lower notes can be written.

The 5th string open is called 'A' and is written here

The 6th string open is called 'E' and is written here

The notes on the 4th, 5th and 6th strings and their positions are shown here:

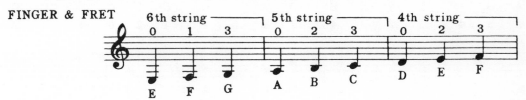

Now try and play 'Clair de Lune' on these strings.

CLAIR DE LUNE

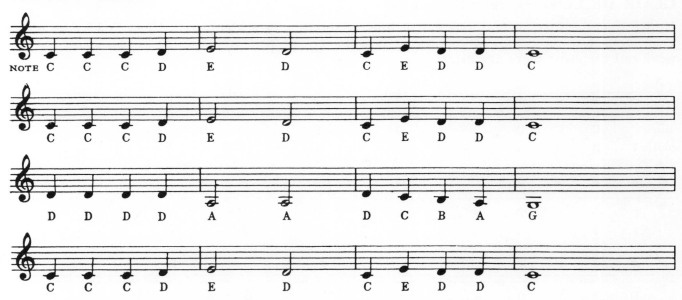

Note: A smooth plectrum technique is obtained by picking the melody notes alternatively down and then upwards.

ALL SIX STRINGS TOGETHER

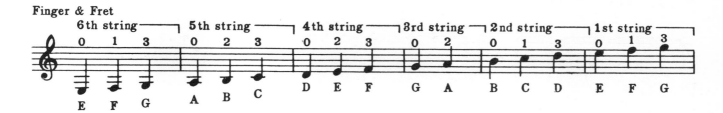

More tunes To Play

The chords, melodies and words are included so that these tunes can be used for chords or melody practice.

JIMMY CRACK CORN

ON TOP OF OLD SMOKEY

The notes tied together (♩. ♩.) are only played once but should sound for their combined time.

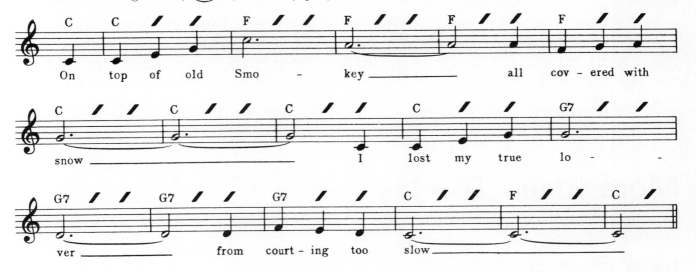

WHEN THE SAINTS GO MARCHING IN

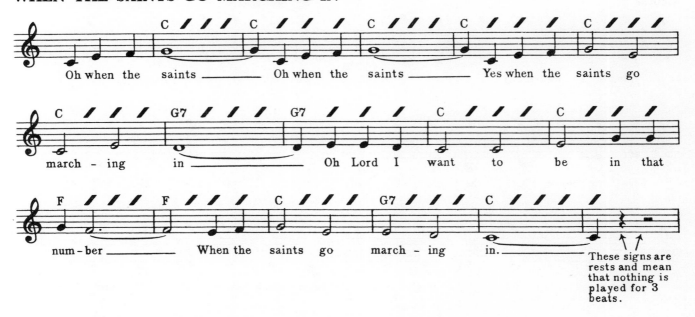

These signs are rests and mean that nothing is played for 3 beats.

FINGERBOARD LAYOUT

These are the notes that you have used so far:

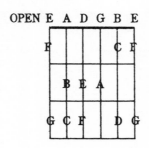

Playing Bass Parts with Chords

When playing chord accompaniments, a bass part can often be added. This will make the accompaniment more interesting, both to play and to listen to.
A bass note can replace one or more of the chord strokes in a bar.
For example, if a 'C' chord is indicated four beats to the bar, the first and third strokes can be replaced by a note 'C' and 'G' respectively:

To play this finger a 'C' chord with the left hand; pick out the 5th string on its own (this is the note 'C') and then play the rest of the chord (the 4th, 3rd, 2nd and 1st strings).
Now pick out the 3rd string on its own—this is the note 'G'—and play the rest of the chord again (this time it will be only the 1st and 2nd strings). Continue playing this until you can do it smoothly.
Usually it is possible to play a bass part using only the notes that are contained in the chords.
In the example below the number of each string is indicated above the note (this will save looking them up if you don't know them yet).

IMPORTANT! ALWAYS FIND THE CHORD BEFORE PICKING OUT THE NOTE.

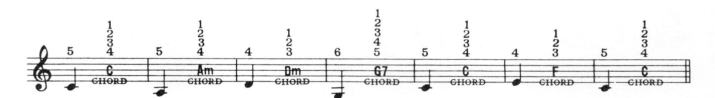

As a chord is a collection of notes on music it would normally be written like this:

This is a five-string 'C' chord. Chords written this way are difficult to read for guitar and so, throughout this book, the chord symbols only are used.

PLECTRUM OR FINGERS?

Playing the bass notes with chords instead of just playing chords on their own brings us to a point about right-hand techniques. This style can be played with a plectrum (on steel strings only) or with the thumb, but if you are interested in developing fingerstyle playing try it this way:
1. Pick out the bass note with the thumb, then
2. Play the rest of the chord by stroking down the strings with the nail of the 1st finger. This is called a 'scratch'.

18

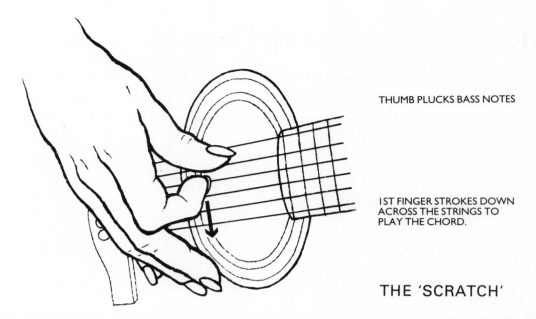

THUMB PLUCKS BASS NOTES

1ST FINGER STROKES DOWN
ACROSS THE STRINGS TO
PLAY THE CHORD.

THE 'SCRATCH'

Played like this the style is called 'Pick and Scratch' or with a plectrum 'Flat Picking'.
Try using either style to accompany this tune in Waltz Time.
Note that there should be two chord strokes after each bass note.

MY BONNIE

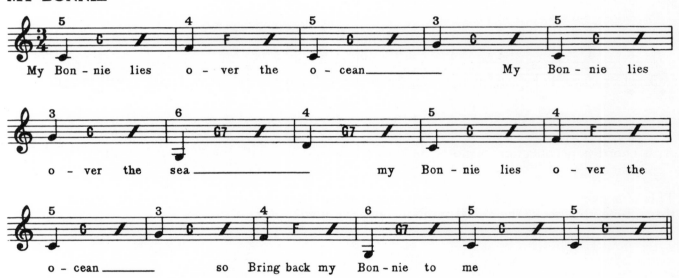

The rest of the tune follows this pattern (which is played twice):

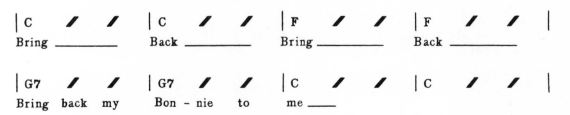

Using the previous part as a guide you should now be able to work out the bass parts for yourself.
By modifying this basic style it is possible to play some melodies and their chords together.

Combining Melody and Chords

This is done by playing the melody note on the first beat (where the bass note has been played up to now) and following it by the chord. Don't forget to find the chord before you play the melody note!

The tune shown below is unusual in that all the melody notes are within the chords—it has been included for this reason, even though it may be unfamiliar to you. Now you can discover the real value of reading music—you can learn to play a tune that you possibly didn't know before. *Note:* The first and third lines are identical!

FOGGY MOUNTAIN TOP

More complicated tunes can be played by adding (or leaving out) notes in the chords. In the next tune it is necessary to add a B flat (B♭) to the 'F' chord in order to play the melody. This note is on the 3rd string at the third fret and is played with the little finger.

The sign (♭) is a symbol to show where a note is flattened—a flat note sounds lower than a normal note.

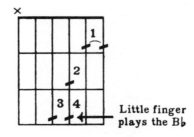

Little finger plays the B♭

Otherwise this tune is no harder to play than 'Foggy Mountain Top'.

JOHN HARDY

DIFFERENT EFFECTS

1. So far, all the 'scratch' strokes have been played down the strings. A different effect can be obtained by playing the bass or melody note and following it with a 'scratch' up. Very fast melodies can be played this way.

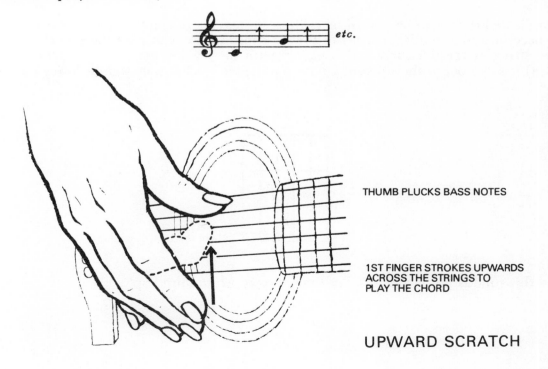

THUMB PLUCKS BASS NOTES

1ST FINGER STROKES UPWARDS
ACROSS THE STRINGS TO
PLAY THE CHORD

UPWARD SCRATCH

The same technique is used with a plectrum (both the single note and the upward scratch are played by it).

2. Another useful technique is to play the single note and then play a scratch up, a scratch down and then another up.

This can be used for accompaniment on its own or with melody. Complicated melodies and bass runs can be played by missing out some of the downstrokes and replacing them with melody or bass notes.

The first part of John Hardy can be improved in this way. The second melody note is found by playing the 4th string open while leaving the rest of the 'C' chord intact.

This could be used at the beginning of the first three lines.

To be really effective this needs to be played quickly and smoothly.

Hammering-On

This is another trick that can make your playing more interesting. It is done by playing a string open and then pushing it on to a fret while it is still sounding (this way two notes are sounded although the string has been picked only once).

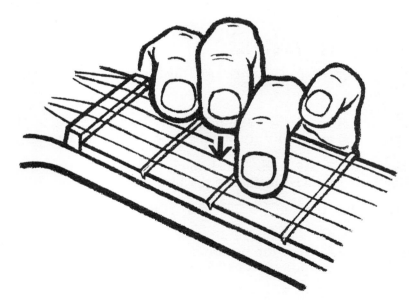

For example, play the 4th string open, then 'hammer' your 2nd finger on to it just behind the second fret. The note 'E' should now sound. This effect can be used on any string and it is sometimes effective to hammer on complete chords. (Try hammering on an 'Am' chord.) When you can hammer-on a single string try using the effect in John Hardy (hammering-on the 'E's' in the fourth line would make the passage more interesting).

More Chords

Notice that different chord shapes produce different sounds.
Compare the difference between chords in the same key, e.g. A, A7, Am.

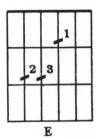

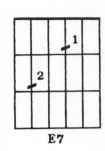

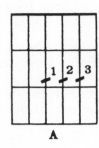

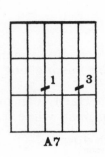

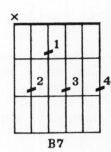

The above chords are often used in 'Twelve Bar Blues' sequences which form the basis of many jazz, folk-blues and pop songs. A typical blues sequence follows:

‖: E / / / | A7 / / / | E / / / | E7 / / / | A / / / | A7 / / / |

| E / / / | E / / / | B7 / / / | A7 / / / | E / A / | E / B7 / :‖ E B7 E — ‖

Abbreviations in Music

In the above sequence some abbreviations, often used in Sheet Music, are shown. (These are to save space and repetition.)

Note the unusual double bar lines at the beginning ‖: and the end :‖ . These mean that on reaching the sign at the end you start playing again from the sign at the beginning.

The sign (¹⎯⎯) over the last bar on the third line is called a '1st time bar'. This means that the first time through the tune is played including the bar, but the second time through this bar is

left out and replaced by the bar marked (²⎯⎯). Other common abbreviations include:

⸹ this means return to a similar sign in the piece of music.
Da Capo or D.C. means start again from the beginning.
Al Coda means go to the Coda. A Coda is an extra piece used to finish off the tune.

⁄. means that the previous bar is to be repeated.
It is as well to be familiar with these signs as they occur quite frequently in single sheets of music in order to save space. The most common are the ones used in the Blues Sequence.

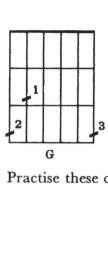 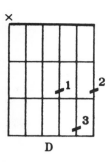 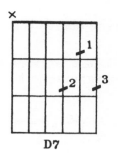 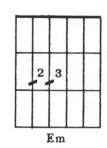 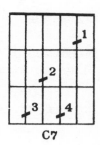

G D D7 Em C7

Practise these chords in these sequences.

1. |G ⁄ C ⁄ |D7 ⁄ G ⁄ |

2. |D ⁄ G ⁄ |A7 ⁄ D ⁄ |

3. |G ⁄ Em ⁄ |Am ⁄ D7 ⁄ |G |

4. |C ⁄ C7 ⁄ |F ⁄ G7 ⁄ |C |

Some of these changes will probably seem a little awkward at first, but all of these chords will be useful.

Although many tunes can be played using only three or four chords, some modern tunes contain many more. It is also necessary when accompanying singing to be able to play in several different keys in order to pitch tunes for different voices.

It's possible to play the chords to a tune in any key, and below are the chords to 'Frankie & Johnny' written in C and G. One of these keys should suit most voices.

FRANKIE AND JOHNNY (in the key of C)

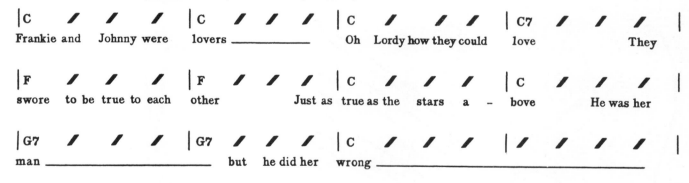

|C ⁄ ⁄ ⁄ |C ⁄ ⁄ ⁄ |C ⁄ ⁄ ⁄ |C7 ⁄ ⁄ ⁄ |
Frankie and Johnny were lovers _____ Oh Lordy how they could love They

|F ⁄ ⁄ ⁄ |F ⁄ ⁄ ⁄ |C ⁄ ⁄ ⁄ |C ⁄ ⁄ ⁄ |
swore to be true to each other Just as true as the stars a – bove He was her

|G7 ⁄ ⁄ ⁄ |G7 ⁄ ⁄ ⁄ |C ⁄ ⁄ ⁄ |⁄ ⁄ ⁄ ⁄ |
man _____ but he did her wrong _____

FRANKIE AND JOHNNY (in the key of G)

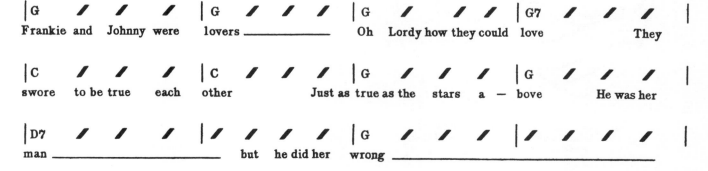

|G ⁄ ⁄ ⁄ |G ⁄ ⁄ ⁄ |G ⁄ ⁄ ⁄ |G7 ⁄ ⁄ ⁄ |
Frankie and Johnny were lovers _____ Oh Lordy how they could love They

|C ⁄ ⁄ ⁄ |C ⁄ ⁄ ⁄ |G ⁄ ⁄ ⁄ |G ⁄ ⁄ ⁄ |
swore to be true each other Just as true as the stars a — bove He was her

|D7 ⁄ ⁄ ⁄ |⁄ ⁄ ⁄ ⁄ |G ⁄ ⁄ ⁄ |⁄ ⁄ ⁄ ⁄ |
man _____ but he did her wrong _____

An example of a sequence containing seven chords is shown below.

NOBODY KNOWS YOU WHEN YOU'RE DOWN AND OUT
(This sequence has also been used for other tunes.)

‖:C ╱ E7 ╱ │A7 ╱ ╱ ╱ │Dm ╱ A7 ╱ │Dm ╱ ╱ ╱ │F ╱ D7 ╱ │C ╱ A7 ╱ │
  5   6   5   6   4   5   4   4   4   5   5

┌1   ┌2
│D7 ╱ ╱ ╱ │G7 ╱ ╱ ╱ :‖ D7 ╱ G7 ╱ │C ╱ A7 ╱ │D7 ╱ G7 ╱ │C G7 C   ‖
  4   5   6   4   4   6   5   5   4   6

The figures underneath are a suggested bass part for these chords.

Some Fingerstyles

Fingerstyles are usually used for accompanying, but certain styles can be adapted for melody playing as well.
It is very important to keep a good right hand position when playing these styles. The maximum control is obtained by picking the strings at a right angle (or as near as possible). A good position is shown below. Fingerpicks can be used, although many people prefer the smoother sound that comes from playing either with the fingernails or with the tips of the fingers. If fingerpicks are used make sure that you wear them the right way round (see drawing).

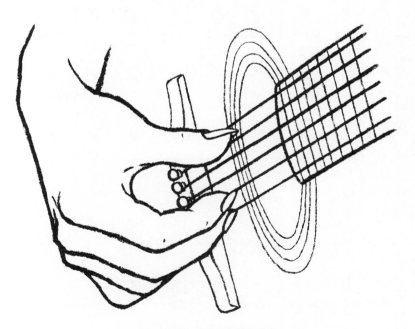

A GOOD RIGHT HAND POSITION
The thumb picks down and the fingers
pluck upwards

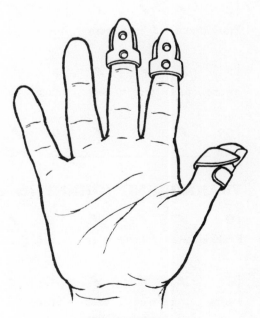

**WEARING FINGER and
THUMB PICKS**
They should be on the
opposite side of the finger
to the nail

DON'T BE PUT OFF—these styles are easier to play than they appear on paper.

FINGERSTYLE NO. 1

In this style the thumb picks the bass note; the 1st finger plucks the 2nd string and the 2nd finger plucks the 1st string. The left hand should finger a 'C' chord.

Stage 1. Pick the 5th string with the thumb.
Stage 2. Pluck the 1st and 2nd strings together (using the fingers mentioned above).
Stage 3. Pick the 3rd string with the thumb.
Stage 4. Pluck the 1st and 2nd strings again.

Written down in music this would be:

THUMB   FINGERS   THUMB   FINGERS

FINGERSTYLE NO. 2

Keeping the fingers in the positions used for style 1, a different effect is obtained by picking each string separately.

First find the 'C' chord.

Stage 1. Pick out the 5th string with the thumb.
Stage 2. Pluck the 2nd string (with the 1st finger).
Stage 3. Pluck the 1st string (with the 2nd finger).
Stage 4. Pick the 3rd string with the thumb.
Stage 5. Pluck the 2nd string again.
Stage 6. Pluck the 1st string again.

This would be written:

Try to play each style smoothly before proceeding to the next.

FINGERSTYLE NO. 3

Adding an extra beat gives another effect.

The fingers should be in the same positions as they were for styles 1 and 2.

Stage 1. Pick the 5th string with the thumb.
Stage 2. Pluck the 2nd string (with the 1st finger).
Stage 3. Pluck the 1st string (with the 2nd finger).
Stage 4. Pluck the 2nd string again.
Stage 5. Pick the 3rd string with the thumb.
Stage 6. Pluck the 2nd string.
Stage 7. Pluck the 1st string.
Stage 8. Pluck the 2nd string again.

This would be written:

This style can be very useful for accompanying slow ballads.

Although all these styles have been shown for the chord of 'C', they can be used with any chords. Refer back to the previous section for the bass notes to other chords.

FINGERSTYLE NO. 4

This is a version of the previous style but in Waltz time. This could be used in 'On Top of Old Smokey' and similar tunes.

Stage 1. Thumb picks 5th string.
Stage 2. 1st finger plucks 2nd string.
Stage 3. 2nd finger plucks 1st string.
Stage 4. Pluck the 2nd string again.
Stage 5. Thumb picks 3rd string.
Stage 6. Pluck 2nd string again.

This is written:

If a second bar is played on the same chord pick the 4th string instead of the 5th string with the thumb (Stage 1).

This would then appear thus:

Variations like this can make a simple, mechanical style sound very effective.

FINGERSTYLE NO. 5

An Arpeggio Style

This time three fingers are used.   The 1st finger plays the 3rd string.
                                     The 2nd finger plays the 2nd string.
                                     The 3rd finger plays the 1st string.
Pick them in this order: The thumb on the bass string, 1st finger, 2nd finger, 3rd finger, 2nd finger, 1st finger and then start again.

FINGERSTYLE NO. 6

In this style the thumb plays a moving part while the fingers play a two-note chord on top.

Stage 1. Pick the 5th string with the thumb.
Stage 2. Pick the 4th string with the thumb.
Stage 3. Pick the 1st and 2nd strings together to make a two-note chord (as in style No. 1).
Stage 4. Pick the 3rd string with the thumb.

This style is useful with a slow number that has a chord change every bar or every other bar.

Clawhammer Styles

In these styles the thumb plays a regular pattern on the bass strings while at the same time the fingers pick out the melody, or another pattern, on the 1st, 2nd and 3rd strings. In all clawhammer playing the pattern played by the thumb should be continuous and on the beat.

BASIC THUMB PATTERNS

1. Find a 'C' chord.
2. Pick the 5th string with the thumb, then
3. Pick the 3rd string with the thumb.

Continue this until it can be played evenly and then find a 'G7' chord. This time pick out the 6th string and then the 4th string with the thumb and practise this until it can be played evenly.

BASIC FINGER AND THUMB PATTERNS

Melodies can be played by the 1st finger while the thumb plays the continuous pattern.

1. Find a 'C' chord.
2. Pick the 5th string with the thumb and at the same time pluck the 1st string with the 1st finger (the thumb should pick downwards while the 1st finger plucks up).

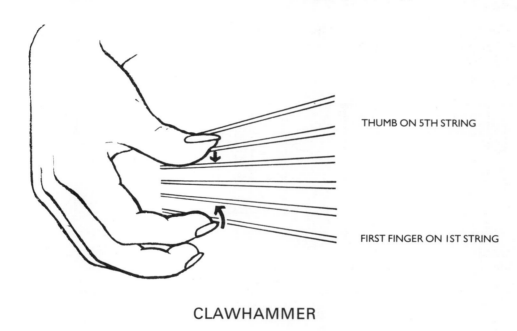

THUMB ON 5TH STRING

FIRST FINGER ON 1ST STRING

CLAWHAMMER

3. Pick the 3rd string with the thumb.
4. Pick the 5th string with the thumb.
5. Pluck the 1st string on its own with the 1st finger.
6. Pick the 3rd string with the thumb.

The timing for this pattern should be:

Chord 'C'	Finger string	1		1	
	Thumb string	5	3	5	3
	Count the beat	1	2	3 and 4	
Chord 'G7'	Finger string	1		1	
	Thumb string	6	4	6	4

When you can play the pattern evenly try this one.

The rhythm is the same and the thumb plays the same strings, but this time use the 1st finger to play the 1st and 2nd strings alternatively.

Chord 'C'	Finger string	1		2	
	Thumb string	5	3	5	3

Count the beat	1	2	3 and 4

Chord 'G7'	Finger string	1		2	
	Thumb string	6	4	6	4

Clawhammer, using the 1st finger and the thumb, is normally called 'two finger style'—the thumb counts as a finger in this case!

Clawhammer Chords

To play melodies it is necessary to modify the chords by adding notes to them (or taking notes out). Some examples are shown below—the usual positions of the melody notes are shown by arrows.

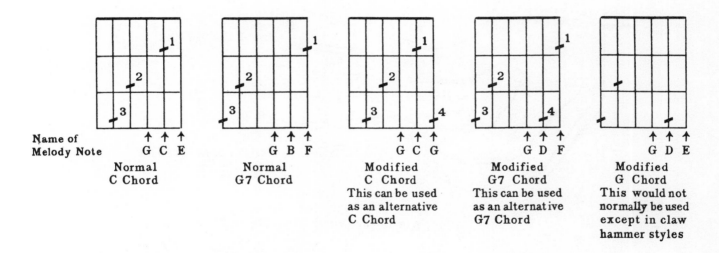

Name of Melody Note	G C E	G B F	G C G	G D F	G D E
	Normal C Chord	Normal G7 Chord	Modified C Chord — This can be used as an alternative C Chord	Modified G7 Chord — This can be used as an alternative G7 Chord	Modified G Chord — This would not normally be used except in claw hammer styles

Using this basic right hand style it is possible to play hundreds of tunes. A simple one using the chords just mentioned is 'Skip to my Lou', which is shown on the next page. This has been written in such a way that it can be played either from the music on the stave or from the chords using the finger and thumb strings indicated. Hold the chord until a change is shown.

SKIP TO MY LOU. Notice that the first and third lines are the same.

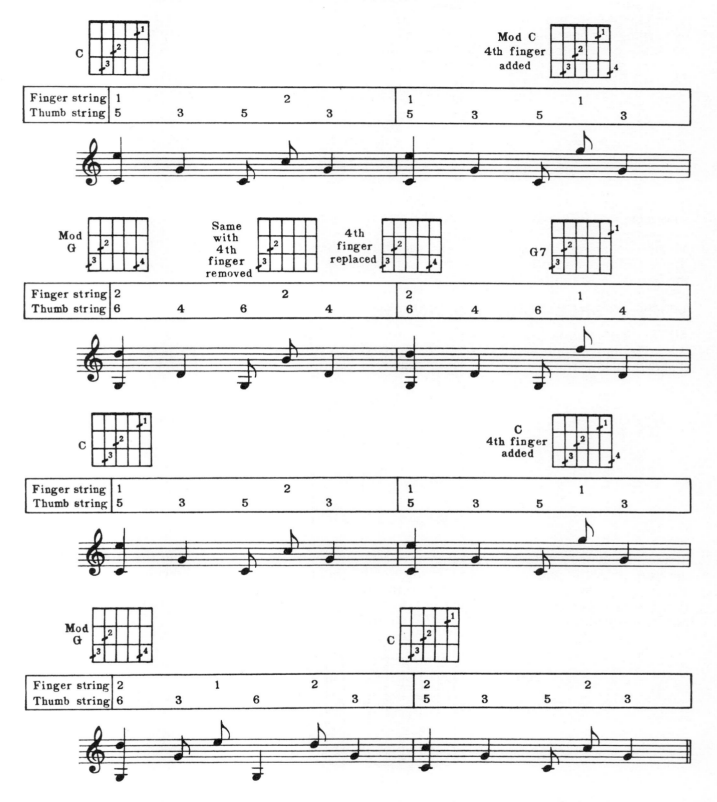

There is an extra note in the bar before the end. This bar should be played to a rhythm of 1, 2 and 3 and 4.

With the exception of this bar the whole of the tune can be played with the basic pattern, which can be automatic. This is all very well, but your playing will sound monotonous if the rhythm is not varied from tune to tune. This can be done, and some more complicated tunes can be played, by varying the position of the notes picked by the fingers. These notes can be played on the beat, at the same time as the notes played by the thumb:

Finger string	1	2	1	2
Thumb string	5	3	5	3
Count the beat	1	2	3	4

or they can be after the note picked by the thumb, in any of the positions shown.

Thumb	5	↓ 3	↓ 5	↓ 3	↓
Count	1 and	2 and	3 and	4 and

The most varied playing would mix the two together.

Melodies that can be played this way include numbers like 'Freight Train', 'Banks of the Ohio', 'Louis Collins', and other folk songs as well as 'oldies', such as 'When You Wore a Tulip', 'When the Saints go Marching In', etc.

MORE CHORDS FOR CLAWHAMMER

All the basic chords (see the chord directory at the back) can be used at one time or another for this style, but certain chords have been evolved specially for clawhammer playing. One of these is shown below and is a type of D7. Melody notes can be played on the 1st, 2nd or 3rd strings.

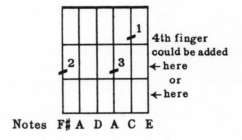

Notes F♯ A D A C E

Besides the melody notes shown different effects can be obtained by removing the 1st finger giving the note B on the 2nd string, hammering this finger on to the position shown, or adding the 4th finger to the 1st string at the second or third fret.
It is common practice when playing in G (another good key for this style) is to use the 'D7' chord just mentioned, and also to play the 'G' chord in one of these two ways.

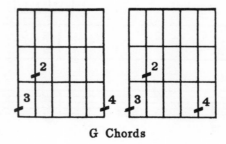

G Chords

The fingering might seem a little awkward but these chords are useful in melody playing and present quick changes to 'G7' and 'C'.

An unusual 'C' chord is also often used with these chords (the bass part played by the thumb would often continue to play 6, 4, 6, 4 through the 'C' chord shown below and also through the 'D7' chord just mentioned).

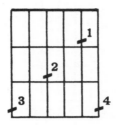

C chord for use in G clawhammer tunes

One problem with playing in 'C' (by far the most common key for this style) is to be able to play a good bass pattern for the 'F' chords which occur. This is usually solved by bringing the thumb round to stop the 6th string at the first fret (see drawing), which enables a 6, 4, 6, 4 bass pattern to be played. If you are unable to do this a 4, 3, 4, 3 or 4, 3, 4 5 pattern can be used but it is not as effective.

This is not recommended for any other style but clawhammer.

Melody notes with the chord of 'F' can be on the 1st, 2nd or 3rd strings. Extra notes can be played by the little finger as shown, or the 1st finger can be removed to play the 1st or 2nd string open.

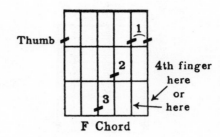

F Chord

Hammering-on is quite common in this style of playing and can be used on any of the strings or with parts of chords, e.g. the 1st and 2nd fingers of the 'C' chord shown previously can be hammered-on.

PULLING OFF NOTES

This is another useful technique and is really the opposite of hammering-on. The effect is usually used on the 1st and 2nd strings.
Try it on a 'C' chord with the little finger on the third fret of the 1st string. Pick the 1st string and then push the little finger across the string and then away. The open note should now sound although the string hasn't been picked a second time.

THREE FINGERED CLAWHAMMER

This is a style using the thumb and the 1st and 2nd fingers (the thumb again counts as a finger). This style will give a much better accompanying sound than the two fingered style dealt with previously.
Again the thumb plays the bass pattern, but this time the 1st finger picks the 2nd string and the 2nd finger picks the 1st string.

Hold a 'C' chord and try it as follows:

Finger string	1	2		1		2	
Thumb string		5	3		5		3
Count the beat	1	and	2	and	3	and	4	etc.

This basic version can be used for playing such tunes as 'Railroad Bill' for melody or accompanying purposes.

If the melody note is on the 2nd string it would be played by the 2nd finger—the 1st finger would move down to the 3rd string. This happens on the 'F' chords and the 'G' chords in the following number. The last bar (a 'C' chord) is also played this way. The 2nd finger should always sound above the rest.

RAILROAD BILL

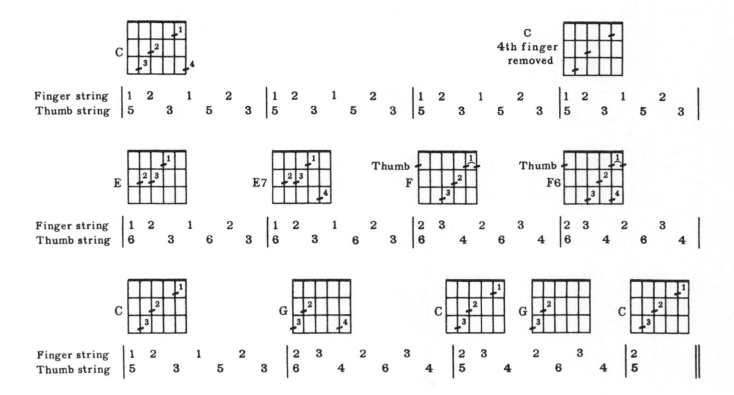

There are many different variations of Clawhammer playing. Some players use a mixture of the two and three finger clawhammer styles for playing melodies (the fast parts of the melody are played by the 1st finger and the 'fill-ins' are played three fingered style, using the 1st and 2nd fingers). Another common three fingered style, shown below, is used in 'Cocaine Blues' and other numbers for melody or accompanying. It is fairly similar to the previous variant, but by adding the extra note on the end of each bar a very different effect is produced.

'COCAINE BLUES' CLAWHAMMER

The thumb pattern is shown for the chord of 'C'. For different chords use the thumb patterns mentioned in previous passages.

Finger String	1 2	1	2	1	2	1	2	1	2	1	2	1	
Thumb String	5 3	5	3	5	3	5	3	5	3	5	3		etc.
Count the beat	1 and 2 and 3 and 4 and	1 and 2 and 3 and 4 and	1 and 2 and 3 and 4 and										

Notice that the 1st bar is different from the rest of the pattern.

More About Music

This section will probably be difficult to remember at first, so keep referring back to it!

SHARPS AND FLATS

So far, most of the melodies in this book have been written without using sharp or flat notes. If you look back to the fingerboard diagram (page 15) you will notice that there are some notes left unnamed. The sharps and flats fit into these positions.

When a note is sharpened it sounds higher than the 'natural' note, if it is flattened it sounds lower. For example, play the note 'G' at the third fret on the 1st string. To play 'G' sharp move onto the fourth fret. 'G' flat is played on the second fret. It is usual to use symbols to indicate sharps and flats.

The sharp sign is ♯.

The flat sign is ♭.

Below the fingerboard has been filled in to show the sharps and flats. Notice that these notes can be called by either sharp or flat names. F sharp (F♯) is the same note as G flat (G♭). Two different names are used to simplify reading and writing melodies—sometimes it is easier in a sharp key and at other times it is easier in a flat key.

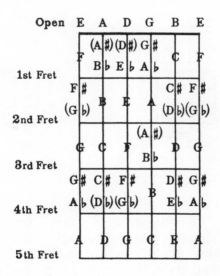

The names in brackets are not used very often but have been included to make this complete.

Note: There is no sharp or flat between 'B' and 'C' or between 'E' and 'F'.

Here the notes are shown on the stave.

THE SHARPS

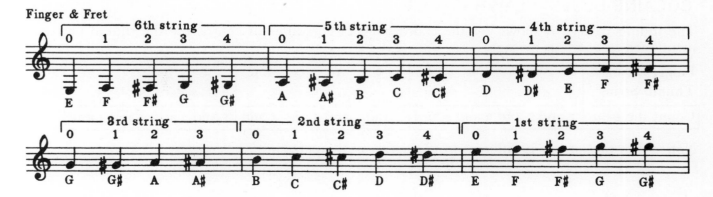

THE FLATS

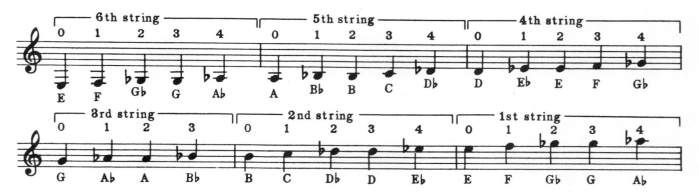

KEY SIGNATURES

At the beginning of each line of a piece of music a key signature is shown. This indicates in which key the melody is written and which sharp or flat notes have to be played. The ♯ or ♭ sign is shown in the position of the note to which it refers, e.g.:

SHARP KEYS

 The sharp sign is written in the position of the note 'F' (shown in brackets). This means that every 'F' must be sharpened. All these notes shown below should be sharpened.

THE FLAT KEYS

 The ♭ sign is written in the position of the note 'B'. This means that every 'B' must be flattened.

COMMON KEY SIGNATURES

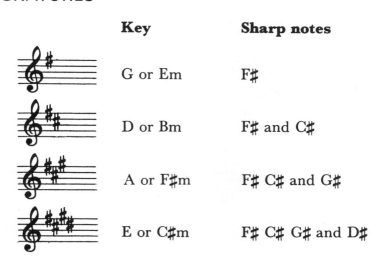

	Key	Sharp notes
	G or Em	F♯
	D or Bm	F♯ and C♯
	A or F♯m	F♯ C♯ and G♯
	E or C♯m	F♯ C♯ G♯ and D♯

	Key	Flat notes
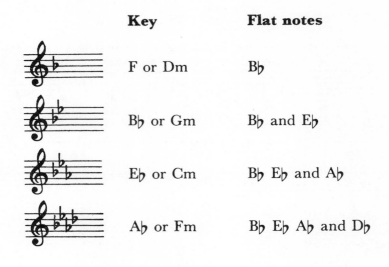	F or Dm	B♭
	B♭ or Gm	B♭ and E♭
	E♭ or Cm	B♭ E♭ and A♭
	A♭ or Fm	B♭ E♭ A♭ and D♭

and finally

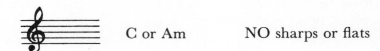

	Key	Flat notes
	C or Am	NO sharps or flats

The key signature can refer to a major or a minor key. The minor key having the same number of sharps or flats as a major key is called the relative minor. Em is the relative minor of G major, and chords of these keys will often be found close together.

NATURAL NOTES

There is one more sign that can affect the note. This is the natural sign (♮), which is used to cancel a sharp or flat which has been indicated in the music. It is only effective for the remainder of the bar after the sign. The melody which follows is in the key of G. (Every F would normally be sharpened.)

Name of note   G   F♮   E   F♮   F♯   E   F♯   G

Note that in the new bar the sharp or flat from the key signature is once again effective.

ACCIDENTALS

These are sharps or flats which aren't in the key signature but occur just for the odd note (like the B♭ which occurred in 'John Hardy').

They work in the same way as naturals and are also only effective for the remainder of the bar. Occasionally 'Accidentals' and 'Naturals' occur in the same bar:

Name of note G   G♯   G♮   F♯   F♮   E

OTHER TIME SIGNATURES

Time signatures earlier on were limited to $\frac{4}{4}$ (Common Time) and $\frac{3}{4}$ (Waltz Time). As mentioned previously, the time signature tells the number and type of beats to each bar.

$\frac{4}{4}$ has four quarter notes (♩) to each bar.

$\frac{3}{4}$ has three quarter notes (♩) to each bar.

There are others, the common ones being:

$\frac{2}{4}$ has two quarter notes to each bar.

$\frac{2}{2}$ has two half notes (♩) to each bar.

$\frac{6}{8}$ has six eighth notes (♪) to each bar.

RESTS are used to indicate places where nothing is to be played. They have time values like the notes they replace and are counted in the same way.

whole note rest   half note rest   quarter note rest   eighth note rest

CHANGING FROM ONE KEY TO ANOTHER—TRANSPOSING

Music isn't always written in the key in which you'd like to play or sing and so it is sometimes necessary to change the key. The easiest way to do this is to compare the scales of the original key and the key to which the melody or chords are to be changed.

The table shown below gives the scales of keys that you are likely to encounter. Minor keys are regarded as being similar to their relative major key.

KEY	SCALE								RELATIVE MINOR
	1	2	3	4	5	6	7	8	
C	C	D	E	F	G	A	B	C	Am
D	D	E	F♯	G	A	B	C♯	D	Bm
E♭	E♭	F	G	A♭	B♭	C	D	E♭	Cm
E	E	F♯	G♯	A	B	C♯	D♯	E	C♯m
F	F	G	A	B♭	C	D	E	F	Dm
G	G	A	B	C	D	E	F♯	G	Em
A♭	A♭	B♭	C	D♭	E♭	F	G	A♭	Fm
A	A	B	C♯	D	E	F♯	G♯	A	F♯m
B♭	B♭	C	D	E♭	F	G	A	B♭	Gm

TRANSPOSING CHORD SEQUENCES

To transpose a chord sequence into a different key you have to decide in which key it is written. This is usually the same as the last chord in the sequence. For example, in the following sequence the last chord is C, and the tune is in C.

| C ╱ G7 ╱ | F ╱ C ╱ | Dm ╱ G7 ╱ | C ╱ G7 ╱ | F ╱ C ╱ | Dm ╱ G7 ╱ | C ╱ ╱ ╱ ‖

Look through the sequence and list the different chords (they only need looking up once each this way) The list is:

C   G7   F   Dm

To change this into the key of D, compare the scale of the original key (C) and the new key (D) on the table above. You will notice that the 1st note in the scale of C is C and the 1st note of the scale of D is D. Therefore a C chord in the sequence will change to a D chord. *Any minors or sevenths must be carried through from one key to the other.*

Comparing the two scales, the next chord (G7) will become A7; the next (F) will become G in the key of D. Carrying through the minor, Dm in the key of C will become Em in the key of D.

Therefore in this sequence every C chord will become a D chord.

> Every G7 chord will become a A7 chord.
> Every F chord will become a G chord.
> Every Dm chord will become a Em chord.

Sequences in minor keys can be transposed the same way.

For example, a sequence in Am might go as follows:

> Am G F E7 Am Dm Am.

This should be looked up under the key of C (its relative major). Change this into the key of Em (which appears under G) by reading the chords off the table.

> Every Am chord would become an Em chord.
> Every G chord would become a D chord.
> Every F chord would become a C chord.
> Every E7 chord would become a B7 chord.
> Every Dm chord would become a Am chord.

On page 22 'Frankie and Johnny' is written in two keys. Use this to check how the chords were changed from one key to another.

TRANSPOSING MELODIES

This works in a similar fashion, but care must be taken to ensure that the melody line is similar in both cases. If it goes up in the original then it must also go up in the changed version.

SHARPS AND FLATS (WHICH ARE NOT IN THE SCALE)

Occasionally notes, or chords, will occur which are not in the scale. If a flat or sharp note which is not in the scale occurs in the original key it must be carried through when you transpose.

For example, a B♭ could occur in the key of C. If you wish to transpose this into D it will mean flattening the corresponding note in the scale of D, which is C♯. The flat will cancel the sharp and the corresponding note will be C natural in the key of D.

AN EXAMPLE WRITTEN IN 3 KEYS

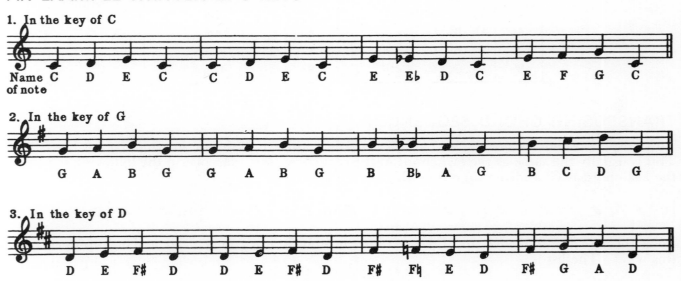

1. In the key of C

Name of note: C D E C C D E C E E♭ D C E F G C

2. In the key of G

G A B G G A B G B B♭ A G B C D G

3. In the key of D

D E F♯ D D E F♯ D F♯ F♮ E D F♯ G A D

Using a 'Capo'

Some effects and styles can only be played using certain chord shapes, e.g. clawhammer, some fingerstyles and flatpicking. By using a capo (the full name is capotasto), it is possible to change the key but still use the same shapes. The capo is clamped down over the strings behind a fret and raises the pitch by shortening the scale of the guitar.

Different Types of Capo's

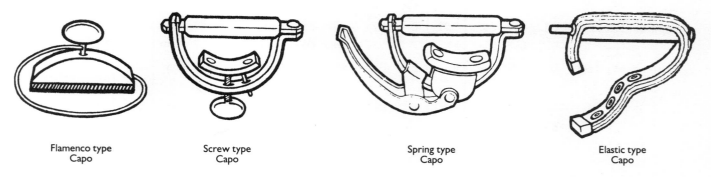

| Flamenco type | Screw type | Spring type | Elastic type |
| Capo | Capo | Capo | Capo |

The original capo was the Flamenco type made of wood and a length of gut. It is still used for Flamenco playing.

The other three types are popular for Folk and Blues playing and have a metal strip covered by a rubber or nylon sleeve which presses against the strings. The screw type is the cheapest to buy but the spring and elastic types are much quicker to move and are favoured by many professional players.

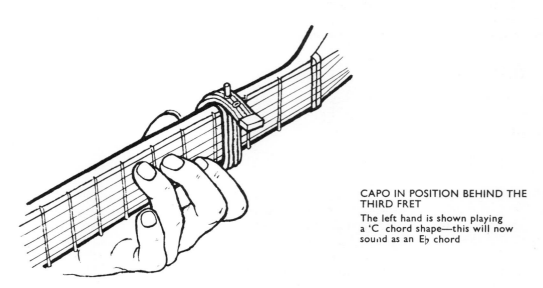

CAPO IN POSITION BEHIND THE THIRD FRET

The left hand is shown playing a 'C' chord shape—this will now sound as an E♭ chord

The name of each chord shape will change depending on the position of the capo, e.g. a sequence in C with the capo at the third fret will actually be in E♭ even though the shapes of C, F, G7, etc., are used.

CHORD NAMES IN DIFFERENT CAPO POSITIONS

Both the flat and sharp names are shown where applicable.

Usual Chord Name (without capo)	A	A7	Am	B7	C	C7	D	D7	Dm	E	E7	Em	F	G	G7
Capo at 1st fret	A♯ / B♭	A♯7 / B♭7	A♯m / B♭m	C7	C♯ / D♭	C♯7 / D♭7	D♯ / E♭	D♯7 / E♭7	D♯m / E♭m	F	F7	Fm	F♯ / G♭	G♯ / A♭	G♯7 / A♭7
Capo at 2nd fret	B	B7	Bm	C♯7 / D♭7	D	D7	E	E7	Em	F♯ / G♭	F♯7 / G♭7	F♯m / G♭m	G	A	A7
Capo at 3rd fret	C	C7	Cm	D7	D♯ / E♭	D♯7 / E♭7	F	F7	Fm	G	G7	Gm	G♯ / A♭	A♯ / B♭	A♯7 / B♭7
Capo at 4th fret	C♯ / D♭	C♯7 / D♭7	C♯m / D♭m	D♯7 / E♭7	E	E7	F♯ / G♭	F♯7 / G♭7	F♯m / G♭m	G♯ / A♭	G♯7 / A♭7	G♯m / A♭m	A	B	B7
Capo at 5th fret	D	D7	Dm	E7	F	F7	G	G7	Gm	A	A7	Am	A♯ / B♭	C	C7
Capo at 6th fret	D♯ / E♭	D♯7 / E♭7	D♯m / E♭m	F7	F♯ / G♭	F♯7 / G♭7	G♯ / A♭	G♯7 / A♭7	G♯m / A♭m	A♯ / B♭	A♯7 / B♭7	A♯m / B♭m	B	C♯ / D♭	C♯7 / D♭7

Different Guitar Tunings

are sometimes used by Folk and Blues musicians to get special effects. The most common one is to tune down the 6th string to D (play the 6th string at the seventh fret and tune down until it is the same as the 5th string open)—and D chords and parts of other chords can be used to play melodies on the top strings while a regular bass pattern is played by the thumb. Care has to be taken with any different tuning as the normal chord shapes will not necessarily apply.

OPEN TUNINGS

With these tunings a chord can be played without the strings being touched by the left hand. Melodies can be added to the chord by fingering one string at a time, although any other chords tend to be rather awkward.

OPEN G TUNING

The usual G tuning is as follows: 1st string is tuned down to D (the same note as the 2nd string at the third fret); the 2nd, 3rd and 4th strings remain in the normal tuning; the 5th string is tuned down to G (the 5th string played at the 7th fret should be the same as the 4th open); and the 6th string is tuned down to D (played at the fifth fret the 6th string should give the same note as the 5th—after tuning). This should result in an open G chord; a C chord would be played by fretting all the strings at the 5th fret (this is done with the 1st finger) and a D chord by fretting all the strings at the 7th fret (also with the 1st finger).

OPEN D TUNING

First tune the 6th string down to D (play the 6th string at the seventh fret and tune down until it is the same as the 5th string open).

The 5th and 4th strings stay the same; tune the 3rd string down to F♯ (the same note as the 4th string at the fourth fret) and then tune the 2nd string down to A (the same note as the 3rd string at the third fret—after tuning to F♯). Tune the 1st string to D by playing the 2nd string at the fifth fret.

A G chord can be played by fretting all the strings at fifth fret and an A chord by fretting them all at the seventh fret.

RE-TUNING

Having played in open tuning, presumably you wish to return to a normal tuning sometime. The 4th string wasn't changed in either the G or D tuning and so the best way is to work up and down from this string.

Tune the 3rd string to the 4th string at the fifth fret, and so on.

There are other open strings, but never use one that raises the pitch of the strings as this will strain the neck of your guitar.

Re-stringing the Guitar

It is advisable to change the strings on a guitar at least every two months, even if the guitar isn't played very much. Old strings will sound 'dead', will drag on the fingers and will tend to strain the neck of the guitar.

Points to remember:

1. Take off one string at a time, leaving the rest tuned up. This will make re-tuning easier and won't strain the neck.

2. Wind the strings on to the machine heads the right way round (see below).

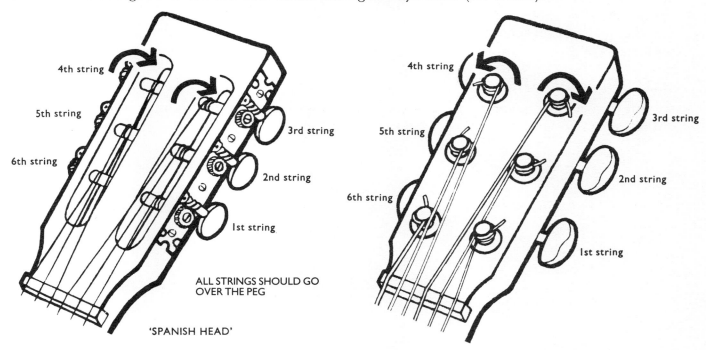

4th string
5th string
6th string
3rd string
2nd string
1st string

ALL STRINGS SHOULD GO OVER THE PEG

'SPANISH HEAD'

4th string
5th string
6th string
3rd string
2nd string
1st string

3. If you use nylon strings put on the 4th, 5th and 6th first, and let them stretch out for a few days, before putting on the other three. Nylon strings always stretch and by doing it this way round the guitar will be easier to keep in tune.

What's Wrong Guide

Sometimes something quite small can affect the sound of your instrument or make it difficult to tune or play. Some of the common faults are analysed here along with their usual remedies. However, if you are in any doubt see an instrument repairer or an experienced musician.

BUZZES AND OTHER VIBRATIONS

1. Check that it isn't just the end of a string rattling.

2. Check that the screws which are used to hold the machine heads in place aren't loose. The mounting screws can be tightened up, but be careful when tightening the screws on the cogs because they could seize up.

3. Have any cracks appeared, or if the bridge is of the fixed type, is it coming away from the face? Neither of these faults is necessarily serious but it is advisable to leave this sort of work to a specialist. Your local music shop will probably be able to recommend one.

4. If one of the strings buzzes it could be that it needs replacing, but if all of them buzz the guitar could be tuned too low (check it with a pitch pipe or another instrument). If this doesn't cure it *don't* tune the guitar higher just to get rid of the buzz—this could permanently damage it. Take the instrument to a repair specialist.

An instrument that is difficult to play should be taken to an instrument repairer as the action may be too high or the frets may be badly worn. These are jobs that require specialised knowledge.

DIFFICULT TO TUNE

1. Check that the bridge is in the right place. The distance from the 12th fret to the nut should be the same as the distance from the 12th fret to the bridge.
If the bridge is of the movable type this can be adjusted, but if the bridge is of the fixed type take the guitar to a specialist.

2. The action could be too high. Some bridges are adjustable for height and these present no problem, the height is raised or lowered by screws. Otherwise this is another job for the repairer.

ELECTRICAL FAULTS

If you have a fault develop in either an amplified guitar or in its amplifier consult a qualified amplifier repair specialist – your local music store can probably recommend someone.

Chord Directory

THE BASIC CHORDS

Note that other chords are to be found under 'Movable Chords' and 'Barre Chords' on pages 46-48.

A

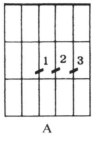

A

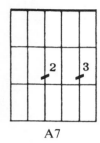

A7

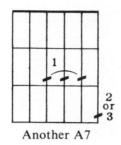

Another A7

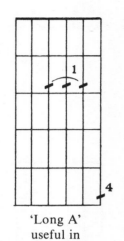

'Long A'
useful in
Blues playing

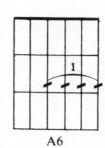

A6

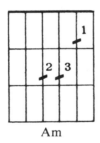

Am

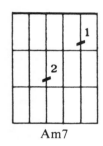

Am7

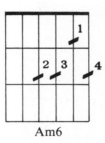

Am6

B

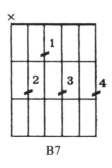

B7

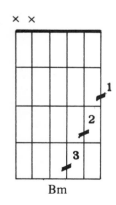

Bm

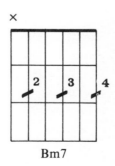

Bm7

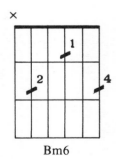

Bm6

44

C

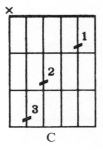
C

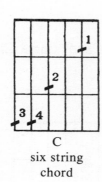
C

six string
chord

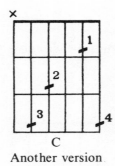
C

Another version

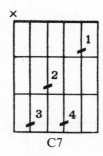
C7

D

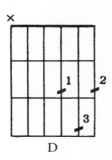
D

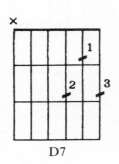
D7

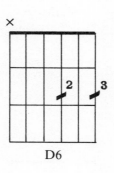
D6

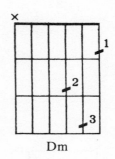
Dm

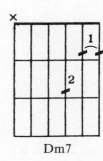
Dm7

E

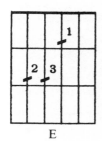
E

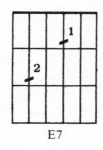
E7

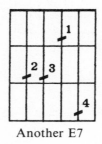
Another E7

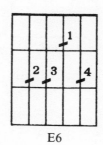
E6

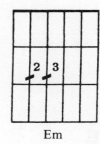
Em

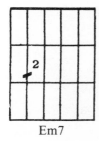
Em7

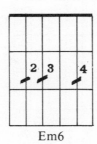
Em6

F

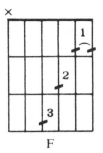

F

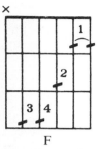

F
(Another version
giving a better
sound)

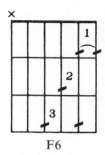

F6

F7
The barre version
is better than this
(see page 48)

Fm
(4 String chord)

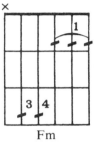

Fm
(5 String chord)

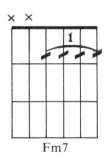

Fm7

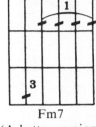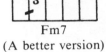

Fm7
(A better version)

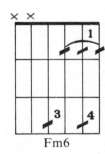

Fm6

G

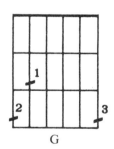

G

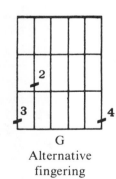

G
Alternative
fingering

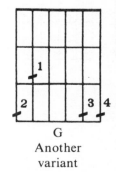

G
Another
variant

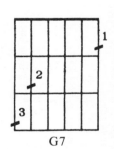

G7

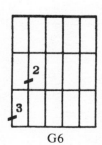

G6

Movable Chords

These are sometimes called 'Closed' chords. Any chord that contains at least four fretted strings can be used in any position as long as any open strings are not played. The position of the chord is named after the fret where the 1st finger plays. If the 1st finger is on the first fret this is the first position and so on.

All the chords below are in the first position but by moving them up the fingerboard they will produce chords of other names as shown.

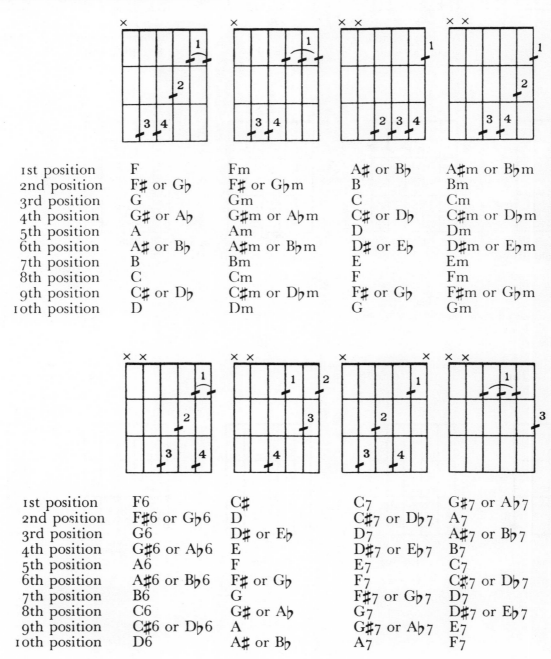

1st position	F	Fm	A♯ or B♭	A♯m or B♭m
2nd position	F♯ or G♭	F♯ or G♭m	B	Bm
3rd position	G	Gm	C	Cm
4th position	G♯ or A♭	G♯m or A♭m	C♯ or D♭	C♯m or D♭m
5th position	A	Am	D	Dm
6th position	A♯ or B♭	A♯m or B♭m	D♯ or E♭	D♯m or E♭m
7th position	B	Bm	E	Em
8th position	C	Cm	F	Fm
9th position	C♯ or D♭	C♯m or D♭m	F♯ or G♭	F♯m or G♭m
10th position	D	Dm	G	Gm

1st position	F6	C♯	C7	G♯7 or A♭7
2nd position	F♯6 or G♭6	D	C♯7 or D♭7	A7
3rd position	G6	D♯ or E♭	D7	A♯7 or B♭7
4th position	G♯6 or A♭6	E	D♯7 or E♭7	B7
5th position	A6	F	E7	C7
6th position	A♯6 or B♭6	F♯ or G♭	F7	C♯7 or D♭7
7th position	B6	G	F♯7 or G♭7	D7
8th position	C6	G♯ or A♭	G7	D♯7 or E♭7
9th position	C♯6 or D♭6	A	G♯7 or A♭7	E7
10th position	D6	A♯ or B♭	A7	F7

The C7 shape (in the third column above) is a particularly useful movable chord. It is necessary to stop the 1st string from sounding. This can be done by just touching it with the 1st finger.

It is possible to play a chord of the same name in several positions, although the notes making up the chord will be in a different order and will give a different effect. These different shapes are called 'inversions'. Generally speaking in rhythm playing it is best to move up and down the fingerboard as little as possible, so choose chords that are close to each other. This will give a balanced rhythm sound.

DIMINISHED CHORDS

These are to be found sometimes in modern music and are indicated like this: Fdim or F°.
Any note in the chord can give its name to the chord—each chord contains four notes and so it can have any of the four names. Either of the chords shown below will fit any key within a few frets.

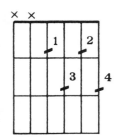   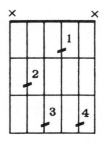

1st position	D♯° or E♭°, A°, C°, F♯° or G♭°	B°, F°, G♯° or A♭°, D°
2nd position	E°, A♯° or B♭°, C♯° or D♭°, G°	C°, F♯° or G♭°, A°, D♯° or E♭°
3rd position	F°, B°, D°, G♯° or A♭°	C♯° or D♭°, G°, A♯° or B♭°, E°

and so on up the fingerboard.

AUGMENTED CHORDS

It is possible to use one chord in most cases where these occur.
Augmented chords are written like this: Caug. or C+
There are three different notes contained in this chord and the name can be taken from any of these.

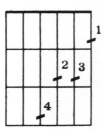

1st position	F+, C♯+ or D♭+, A+
2nd position	F♯+ or G♭+, D+, A♯+ or B♭+
3rd position	G+, D♯+ or E♭+, B+
4th position	G♯+ or A♭+, E+, C+

and so on.

Barré Chords

By using the 1st finger across all strings many movable six string chords can be made. These may seem a bit awkward at first but the bigger sound produced by them makes the effort worthwhile.

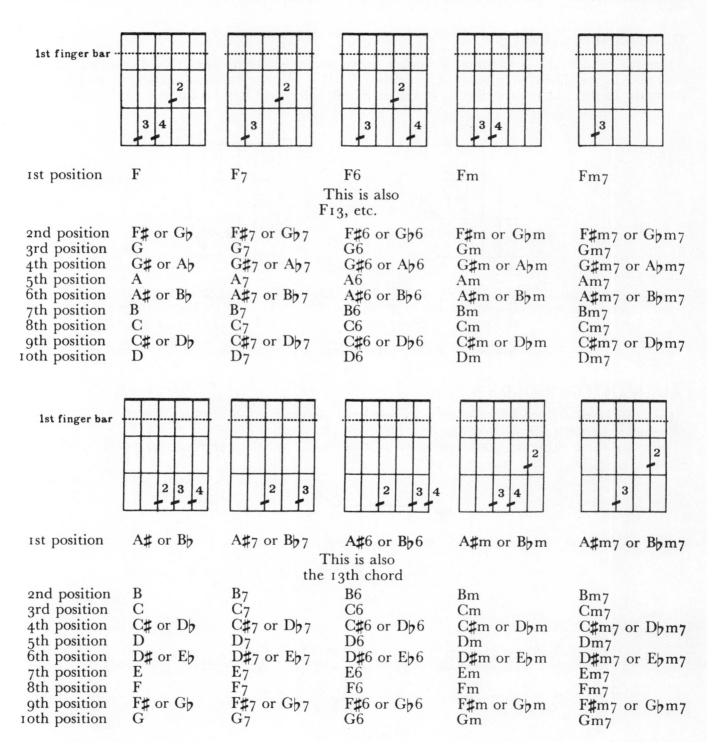

1st position	F	F7	F6	Fm	Fm7

This is also
F13, etc.

2nd position	F♯ or G♭	F♯7 or G♭7	F♯6 or G♭6	F♯m or G♭m	F♯m7 or G♭m7
3rd position	G	G7	G6	Gm	Gm7
4th position	G♯ or A♭	G♯7 or A♭7	G♯6 or A♭6	G♯m or A♭m	G♯m7 or A♭m7
5th position	A	A7	A6	Am	Am7
6th position	A♯ or B♭	A♯7 or B♭7	A♯6 or B♭6	A♯m or B♭m	A♯m7 or B♭m7
7th position	B	B7	B6	Bm	Bm7
8th position	C	C7	C6	Cm	Cm7
9th position	C♯ or D♭	C♯7 or D♭7	C♯6 or D♭6	C♯m or D♭m	C♯m7 or D♭m7
10th position	D	D7	D6	Dm	Dm7

1st position	A♯ or B♭	A♯7 or B♭7	A♯6 or B♭6	A♯m or B♭m	A♯m7 or B♭m7

This is also
the 13th chord

2nd position	B	B7	B6	Bm	Bm7
3rd position	C	C7	C6	Cm	Cm7
4th position	C♯ or D♭	C♯7 or D♭7	C♯6 or D♭6	C♯m or D♭m	C♯m7 or D♭m7
5th position	D	D7	D6	Dm	Dm7
6th position	D♯ or E♭	D♯7 or E♭7	D♯6 or E♭6	D♯m or E♭m	D♯m7 or E♭m7
7th position	E	E7	E6	Em	Em7
8th position	F	F7	F6	Fm	Fm7
9th position	F♯ or G♭	F♯7 or G♭7	F♯6 or G♭6	F♯m or G♭m	F♯m7 or G♭m7
10th position	G	G7	G6	Gm	Gm7

In barré chords the 1st finger is used to replace the nut of the guitar—in the same way as a capo. Other barré chords can be made up by playing open chord shapes above the 1st finger bar.

SIMPLIFYING DIFFICULT CHORD SEQUENCES

Some times in sheet music a chord sequence will appear that is extremely difficult to perform on the guitar. These parts are often written with the piano in mind and they can be simplified for guitar. Generally speaking an ordinary major chord can be used instead of 6th, 7th, 9th chords, etc., although if an augmented or diminished appears it should be played:

A C chord could replace C6, C7, C9, C13, etc., although a C7 would be better to replace a C9 or C13.

A Cm chord could replace Cm6, Cm7, Cm9, etc.

A Cdim. chord could replace C7$\flat$5 (also written C7-5).

A Caug. chord could replace C7+ (sometimes written C7$\sharp$5).

These substitutions can be used in other keys in the same way.
If, however, you wish to play jazz or dance band styles it is as well to learn as many chords as possible. The 6th, 9th, 13th, etc., chords are used to make the harmony of a piece more interesting and should really be played, if possible.

Complete Fingerboard Layout

GOING ON FROM HERE

There is still a lot to learn in whatever style or styles you play. Listen to and watch as many guitarists as possible, and try to work out how they play music which pleases you. A great deal can be learned this way once the first principles of playing have been mastered.

Look for guitar books and books of music at your local music shop, so you can continue to learn to play new music and have fun playing the guitar.

More Tunes for Practising

CARELESS LOVE
(Can be played bass and chords, chords alone, melody and chords or fingerstyle Nos. 1, 3 or 6.)

Love oh love, oh, care - less love _____ Love oh,

love oh, care - less love _____ Love oh love oh

care - less love Just see what love has done to me. _____

FRANKIE AND JOHNNY
(Chords, bass and chords or three-finger clawhammer accompaniment.)

Fran - kie and John - ny were lo - vers Oh lor - dy how they could love. They

swore to be true to each oth - er Just as true as the stars a -

bove. He was her man but he did her wrong _____

THE FOGGY, FOGGY DEW
(Accompaniment: chords alone, bass and chords, fingerstyles 3 or 6.)

When I was a bach-el-or I lived by my-self and I worked in the wea-vers trade The

on-ly thing I did that was wrong was to woo a fair young maid I wooed her in the

sum-mer time and in the win-ter too___ and the on-ly on-ly thing I

did that was wrong was to keep her from the fog-gy fog-gy dew.

GREENSLEEVES
(Accompaniment: chords, bass and chords, fingerstyles 4 and 5 and with some ingenuity the melody can be played clawhammer two-finger style.)

A - las my love___ you do me wrong to___ cast me off so dis-court-eous - ly, When

I have loved___ you oh___ so long___ de - light - ing in___ your com - pan - y

Green - sleeves was all my joy___ and Green - sleeves was my de - light

Green - sleeves was my heart of gold___ and who but my la - dy Green - sleeves

Printed by
Halstan & Co. Ltd., Amersham, Bucks., England